Dangerous DINING

Rob Waring, *Series Editor*

HEINLE
CENGAGE Learning™

Australia • Brazil • Japan • Korea • Mexico • Singapore • Spain • United Kingdom • United States

Words to Know

This story is set in the country of Japan. It happens in the city of Tokyo.

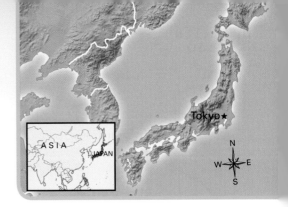

A Dangerous Fish. Read the paragraph. Then complete the sentences with the correct form of the <u>underlined</u> words.

The Tsukiji [skidʒi] <u>seafood</u> market is one of the best places in Tokyo to buy fresh fish. One of the most expensive fish there is the famous—and dangerous—<u>puffer fish</u>, or as the Japanese call it, *fugu*. Parts of the puffer fish's body are full of <u>poison</u> and people can die from eating them. Despite this, there are many restaurants where <u>diners</u> can eat *fugu*. <u>Dining on</u> *fugu* in these restaurants is usually safe. They have special <u>chefs</u> who have learned how to prepare the fish correctly. These chefs have a <u>license</u> that allows them to prepare and serve puffer fish.

1. A _____ is an official document that allows you to do or have something.

2. A _____ is a skilled cook who works in a restaurant.

3. A _____ is a kind of fish.

4. _____ is a polite way to say 'eat'.

5. A _____ is a material that can make you ill or kill you if you eat or drink it.

6. _____ refers to sea animals eaten as food.

7. A _____ is someone who is eating in a restaurant.

B **Poison!** Read the paragraph, then look at the pictures. Write the correct item number next to each word in **bold**.

Puffer fish breathe through **gills** ( ) as their **heart** ( ) moves blood through their body. These parts of the puffer fish are full of poison, but the main part of the fish, or **flesh** ( ), is eaten in Japan. Traditionally, the **fin** ( ), or the part of the fish which helps it to swim, is served in *sake*, a Japanese drink. If a person eats puffer fish poison, it damages their **nerves** ( ) so that they can't move. This damage also affects the **lungs** ( ), which may fail and result in death.

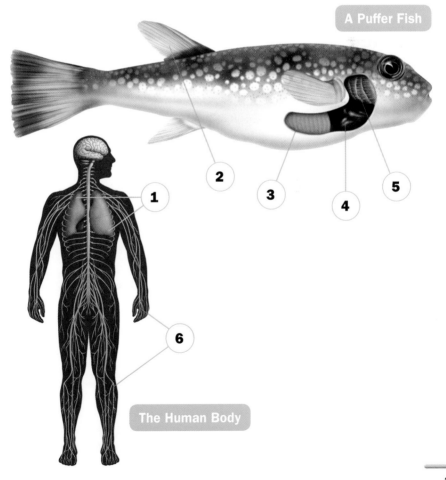

A Puffer Fish

The Human Body

Fish is one of the major foods that people eat in the country of Japan. Every morning, thousands of fish sellers crowd the famous Tsukiji seafood market in Tokyo. Tsukiji is one of the best places in the city to buy fish. Here, no product has a higher price than the one product that's also the most dangerous—the puffer fish.

People who eat this extremely poisonous fish are playing a dangerous game. If they lose the game and get a piece of fish that has poison in it, they may die! This fish is the one that Japanese people call '*fugu*.'

CD 2, Track 09

Despite the danger, *fugu* appears on more than 80 menus in the **Asakusa**[1] restaurant area of Tokyo. This fish is so ugly that it's almost cute, but the puffer fish doesn't fool most diners. They know just how dangerous it is, and most of them are actually happy to challenge the danger of eating this food.

Tom Caradonna is one of these diners. He's visiting Tokyo because he wants to have the complete *fugu* experience, and he's brought his friend, Aki. Wisely, Tom has chosen to eat at the famous Matsumoto restaurant. This *fugu* restaurant is 120 years old and it's well known for its careful preparation of puffer fish. That's very important when you're taking risks with a **toxin**[2] which is 1,000 times stronger than **cyanide**![3]

---

[1] **Asakusa:** [asakusa]
[2] **toxin:** poisonous material
[3] **cyanide:** one of the world's strongest and deadliest poisons

How does Tom feel before dining on this dangerous fish? It seems he's not too worried. He and Aki happily go into the Matsumoto restaurant to try *fugu* for the first time. As he sits down at the table, Tom says: "I've heard stories about people dying by trying the *fugu*, but it hasn't really concerned me." Even though Tom isn't too scared to try *fugu*, there is a big risk. Over the years, hundreds of people have died from eating puffer fish.

At the Matsumoto restaurant, Chef **Hayashi**[4] is the one who will serve Tom his first *fugu*. He's also the one who must prepare the fish safely so that Tom and Aki don't get sick. Luckily, Chef Hayashi really knows what he's doing; he's been preparing *fugu* for a very long time. He comes to meet Tom at the table before he prepares the meal. As he shows Tom his *fugu* preparation license, he says: "It'll be fine, don't worry. I've been doing this for 53 years. I took the exam in 1949 and passed it." He then shows Tom the small piece of paper and says proudly, "This is my *fugu* chef license."

---

[4]**Hayashi:** [hayaʃi]

Scan for Information

Scan pages 11 and 12 to answer these questions.

1. Who created the first regulations for *fugu* preparation?

2. How many people died from *fugu* poisoning between 1945 and 1975?

3. These days, how many people die from *fugu* poisoning every year?

4. What percentage of poisonings happen at home?

1949 was a long time ago, but it was a time when a lot of chefs got their *fugu* license. After World War II, there were many, many deaths from eating *fugu*. Many Japanese people were very hungry, and some looked for food in restaurant trash that was outside on the street. Sometimes these people found *fugu* which had been thrown out. When they cooked and ate the pieces of *fugu*, they got sick or died.

The problem of people getting sick from eating *fugu* became very serious. Eventually, American **General**[5] Douglas MacArthur, who led the U.S. forces in Japan, created **strict**[6] controls and regulations. *Fugu* chefs had to get licenses, and it's been the same ever since that time. If a chef doesn't have a license, he or she cannot serve puffer fish.

---

[5]**General:** an officer with a very high rank, or level, especially in the armed forces
[6]**strict:** strong; very limiting

Even with more regulations, *fugu* killed 2,500 Japanese people between 1945 and 1975. Since then, things have improved. Regulations and education have cut the number of deaths to only three annually, but many diners still get sick.

Hidenori Kadobayashi is a representative from the Tokyo health department. He explains that nowadays most problems happen at home, not at restaurants. "About 70 percent of the poisonings happen in private homes," he says, "where people catch and prepare *fugu* on their own and get poisoned. That's most common." *Fugu* is certainly dangerous, so what are scientists doing to stop people from getting sick if they eat poisoned fish?

At the Tokyo **University of Fisheries**,[7] Yuji Nagashima studies *fugu* poison carefully. He hopes to develop an anti-toxin, which is a medicine that will stop people from dying because of *fugu* poisoning. Nagashima talks about the fish, which is also called the 'tiger *fugu*.' He says: "A tiger *fugu* has enough toxin to kill 30 people. The toxin itself, to give you an idea, is 1,000 times stronger than cyanide."

Fugu toxin is a very strong poison. In fact, one milligram of the toxin is strong enough to kill a person. It kills by **paralyzing**[8] people's nerves. This means that the person who has been poisoned can't move. It also paralyzes the lungs so that the person can't breathe. The only way to save them is to use a respirator, which is a special machine that breathes for the person. They must stay on the respirator until the toxin **wears off**.[9]

---

[7] **University of Fisheries:** a university for the study of fish and fish-related businesses
[8] **paralyze:** cause something to lose the ability to move or feel
[9] **wear off:** disappear little by little

Back in the Matsumoto restaurant kitchen, Chef Hayashi is preparing the *fugu* for Tom and Aki. He explains what each piece is as he cuts through the fish. "This is the heart," he says as he points to a small round part. "These are the gills," he says as he puts a large mass on a plate. "They're poison," he warns.

Toxins make about half of the puffer impossible to eat. Chef Hayashi carefully cuts away the poisonous parts of the fish and throws them out. Then, he cuts the remaining flesh very thinly. Finally, he places the *fugu* on a plate and puts it in the shape of a **chrysanthemum**.[10] The chrysanthemum is a beautiful flower that's popular in Japan. Appropriately for a *fugu* meal, it's also a common flower at **funerals**.[11]

---

[10] **chrysanthemum:** [krɪsænθəməm]
[11] **funeral:** service that is held when a person dies

Chefs usually place the fugu *flesh in the shape of a chrysanthemum, a flower commonly seen at funerals.*

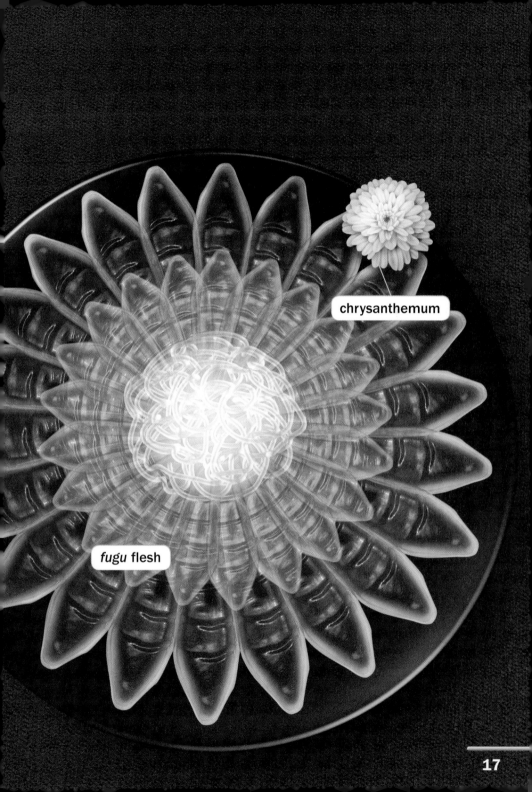

chrysanthemum

fugu flesh

At the table, Aki and Tom are ready to try the freshly prepared *fugu*. When the fish arrives, Tom laughs nervously as he picks it up. He puts it in his mouth and then smiles. "Still breathing?" asks Aki. "I can still breathe!" replies Tom and he continues his meal.

A *fugu* meal is usually eight different dishes. These dishes feature *fugu* that is prepared in different ways. Later, Chef Hayashi brings out two glasses that are filled with *sake* and topped with a cooked *fugu* fin. As the Chef lights the *sake* on fire, Aki and Tom are very impressed. Tom's favorite course is the **grilled**[12] *fugu*, and Aki agrees. At the end of the meal, Tom smiles; he's happy that he's still healthy and breathing.

The puffer fish may be dangerous, but for some, it's a delicious meal. Many people wouldn't even try a dinner that could kill them. Luckily Tom has survived his dangerous dining experience— at least this time!

---

[12] **grilled:** (food) cooked by direct heat

What do you think?

1. Did Tom do the right thing by trying the puffer fish? Why or why not?

2. Would you try it? Why or why not?

After You Read

1. Which is a suitable heading for paragraph 1 on page 4?
   A. People Always Die from Puffer Fish
   B. Deadly Fish Expensive to Buy
   C. Market Famous for Selling Tsukiji
   D. Japanese People Eat Too Much

2. In paragraph 1 on page 7, the word 'challenge' can be replaced by:
   A. taste
   B. stop
   C. refuse
   D. test

3. The writer thinks that Matsumoto restaurant:
   A. makes delicious puffer fish
   B. is over 200 years old
   C. has a lot of foreign tourists
   D. is a good place to go for puffer fish

4. Why does the writer give details about how many people died from *fugu*?
   A. to show that eating puffer fish is not always safe
   B. to show that Tom should not be worried
   C. to show that some people are unlucky
   D. to show that Tom is unhappy

5. In paragraph 2 on page 8, 'it' in 'passed it' refers to a:
   A. license
   B. fish
   C. test
   D. chef

6. Which of the following is NOT a reason that chefs had to get licenses?
   A. An American General made regulations.
   B. No one knew how to cook puffer fish.
   C. People died from eating puffer fish.
   D. Puffer fish must be prepared safely.

7. Some people ate puffer fish out _____ the trash.
   A. of
   B. from
   C. to
   D. on

8. Which is NOT a reason why people died from *fugu* before 1945?
   A. There was no education about *fugu* preparation.
   B. The preparation was incorrect.
   C. There were no regulations for *fugu* preparation.
   D. There were poisonous plates.

9. What's a good heading for page 15?
   A. Scientist Studies Poison
   B. Better than Cyanide
   C. Scientist Cures Victim
   D. Thirty People Die

10. In paragraph 1 on page 16, the word 'mass' means a:
   A. shape
   B. weight
   C. heart
   D. a solid piece

11. What is Aki's favorite type of *fugu*?
   A. fresh
   B. in *sake*
   C. grilled
   D. cold

12. How does the writer probably feel about eating puffer fish?
   A. It's very safe.
   B. It's a little unusual.
   C. It's too dangerous to eat.
   D. It's a healthy meal.

Ask Dr. Jeffers

This month Dr. Jeffers is answering questions about stomach pain and food-related sicknesses.

DEAR DR. JEFFERS,

Recently, I visited some friends in another city. While I was on the trip, I ate some delicious seafood with them in a very nice restaurant. (I had the grilled fish.) After lunch, I began to feel really sick. Eventually, I had to go back to my hotel to rest. Soon my stomach really hurt! The pain lasted for about two hours, but then it wore off. I talked to the other diners who ate lunch with me, however none of them felt sick. Do you think it was food poisoning? Does food poisoning go away that quickly?

—Annie Jacobs, Montreal, Quebec, Canada

Common Food-Related Sicknesses—What to Do

Signs	Possible Causes	Action
• slight stomach pain after eating • continues for two hours or less	• eating too much • eating too fast	• rest in bed or in a chair • put hot cloths on the stomach area
• bad stomach pain continuing more than four hours • stomach pain that wakes you up in the night • stomach pain with a temperature above 101° F	• food poisoning • a non-food related illness such as the flu	• call your doctor and describe the pain to him/her OR • go to the nearest hospital

DEAR MS. JACOBS,

Sometimes food poisoning does go away rather quickly. However, it's not a good idea to wait for this to happen. Food poisoning can be a very serious condition. In my opinion, you probably just ate too much, or ate too fast. People sometimes do that when food tastes really good.

Food poisoning happens when you consume food that contains toxins. These toxins can come from the food itself or from the hands of the people who prepared it. Food poisoning can be very dangerous. I've created a chart to show the differences between regular stomach pain and food poisoning. I hope this helps.

—Dr. J.

CD 2, Track 10

Word Count: 320
Time: _____

Vocabulary List

chef (2, 8, 11, 16, 18)
chrysanthemum (16, 17)
cyanide (7, 15)
dine on (2, 8)
diner (2, 7, 12)
fin (3, 18)
flesh (3, 16, 17)
funeral (16)
General (11)
gill (3, 16)
grilled (18)
heart (3, 16)
license (2, 8, 11)
lung (3, 15)
nerve (3, 15)
paralyze (15)
poison (2, 3, 4, 9, 12, 15, 16)
puffer fish (2, 3, 4, 7, 8, 11, 16, 18, 19)
seafood (2, 4)
strict (11)
toxin (7, 15, 16)
wear off (15)